A GUIDE TO SOFT CLAY ART

CLAY ART
for all seasons

Yukiko Miyai

ISLAND HERITAGE™
PUBLISHING

ISLAND HERITAGE™
P U B L I S H I N G
A DIVISION OF THE MADDEN CORPORATION

94-411 KŌʻAKI STREET, WAIPAHU, HAWAIʻI 96797-2806
Orders: (800) 468-2800 • Information: (808) 564-8800
Fax: (808) 564-8877
islandheritage.com

ISBN: 1-59700-256-9
First Edition, Third Printing, 2008

Photography by: Rachel Robertson
                 Roméo Collado

Location shoot: The Bayer Estate

Acknowledgments

Since I started working with my mother, I have discovered so much about myself and my creative side. Working with this unique air-dry clay inspires me everyday to keep creating, and each day I am inspired by the beautiful sky, mountains, ocean, rainbows and flowers that surround me in Hawai'i.

I feel very privileged to have worked with so many talented people who helped me publish this book. I would first like to thank Island Heritage for giving me the opportunity to share this new art. It is my pleasure to work with their wonderful staff.

I would also like to thank Rachel Robertson, a very talented photographer. Her excellent photographs make this book so unique and fun. And thank you very much to Roméo Collado for his wonderful work.

To my staff at the studio—Ken Fasioen-Delbeek for her creative vision and attention to detail; Margaret Wong for carrying me through all the hurdles and keeping my business going in the right direction; Marlo Tajiri for always doing so much more than I ask of her. I cannot thank you all enough.

I would also like to thank all the people who have supported me during this past year. I couldn't have come this far without you. Thank you very much!!!

My family and friends have been a big support throughout my life, and I would like to say a very special thank you to my parents who are always there for me.

Yukiko Miyai

Table of Contents

Introduction

In the world of decorative clay arts, ClayCraft™ by Deco® is the gold medal winner. This innovative air-dried modeling clay—light, pliable, easy to work with, and versatile—is ideal for all projects, from the simplest to the most imaginative. It can be fashioned into any shape, including ultra-thin and delicate pieces; endless color mixing possibilities make it perfect for detail work.

Finished creations are not only beautiful, they are lightweight and soft to the touch, yet exceptionally durable for a lifetime of enjoyment.

This unique clay product was developed in Japan by my mother, Kazuko Miyai. In 1981, her passion for crafting inspired her to work with a chemist to develop a perfect clay. When she was finally satisfied with the results, she began doing presentations and conducting workshops to share her love of clay crafting.

Since then, she has authored more than twenty craft books, and she continues to develop and enhance her unique techniques to ever more sophistication and complexity. She also actively exhibits her works each year and shares her new techniques with audiences abroad; in addition, she has certified two thousand instructors across Japan, Hong Kong and Taiwan.

After training under my mother, I brought ClayCraft by Deco to Hawai'i in 2000 and founded Deco Clay Craft Academy. Since then, we have expanded throughout the state as well as to California, sharing our distinctive art form with an ever-widening audience. For more information, please visit the Deco Clay Craft Academy website at decoclay.com.

Making your own beautiful accent pieces with ClayCraft by Deco is easy to learn—and they will bring you enjoyment for years to come. So let's get started!

Yukiko Miyai

Getting Started

BASIC MATERIALS AND TOOLS

ClayCraft by Deco soft clay comes in seven colors—white, red, yellow, blue, black, green, and brown. These basic colors can be mixed to create the exact colors you want for your own unique creations. See Color Chart on page 12 for mixing guidelines.

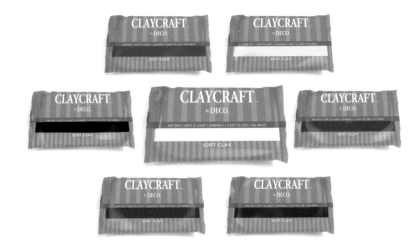

BASIC TOOLS

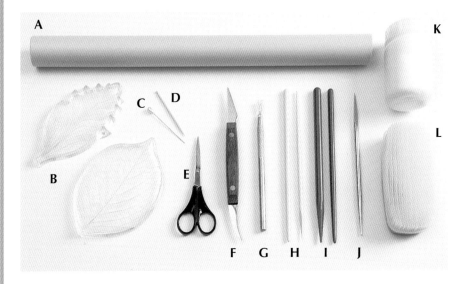

Tools: These items will make working with the clay simple and easy.

A Roller: to flatten and stretch the clay
B Leaf Molds: to make leaves and petals with
C Corsage Pin: for intricate details such as patterns on the clay surface
D Toothpick: to roll out small petals
E Scissors: to cut off excess clay, cut and separate petals and for detail
F Cutter: to cut the clay
G Texture Brush: to add lines, marks or texture
H Deco Detail Sticks: for creating petals and texture
I Detail Sticks: for creating petals and texture
J Metal Detail Stick: for creating petals and texture
K Glue: for attaching clay pieces to other material
L Plastic Texture Brush: to add texture to clay

ADDITIONAL TOOLS AND MATERIALS

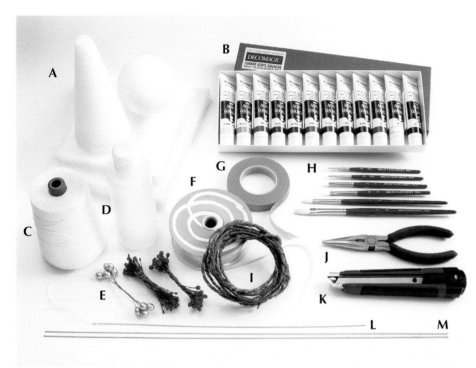

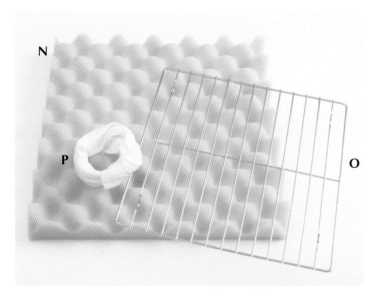

A Styrofoam Forms: used as a base for large projects

B Deco Acrylic Set: to add accent to your pieces

C Cotton String: to string lei

D Water-based Glue: for clay on clay attachment

E Artificial Stamens: for use with some flowers

F Ribbon: used as a finishing touch to your projects

G Floral Tape: to cover exposed wires attached to some flowers

H Deco Paintbrushes: use with Deco Acrylic Set

I Artificial Vine: used as a finishing touch to some projects

J Long Nose Pliers/Wire Cutter: to cut wires

K Box Cutter: to cut Styrofoam and thicker pieces of dried clay

L Lei Needle: to string flowers for lei

M Floral Wire: used to make stems, hairpicks and for arrangements.

N Egg Crate Foam: used as a soft surface to dry flowers

O Cooling Rack: used to dry flowers with large petals

P Paper Towel Ring: used to dry flowers with large or long petals

WORKING WITH THE CLAY

Follow these simple guidelines to make working with ClayCraft by Deco easy:
- Begin by briefly kneading the clay between your fingers to soften it.
  (Be sure not to over-knead as this can make the clay too stiff.)
- Work on a flat, non-absorbent surface that will preserve the clay's moisture.
- If the clay becomes too dry, add in a little fresh, soft clay, or add a few drops of water to restore its softness and pliability.
- As you finish the various sections of your piece, keep them moist so they will stick together during final assembly. Do this by moistening paper towels and covering your unused clay and "parts" of your unfinished projects.
- Air-dry your completed item. The average drying times are half a day for the outer surface and one to two days for the item to dry completely, although this can vary according to climate. Depending on the size and shape of the item, you can set items to dry on paper towels tied into rings, bumpy-surfaced sponges, metal baking racks, or egg cartons.
- If desired, you may add paint to your finished item, or you may brush on a light coat of varnish to add sheen and also prevent discoloration.
- Wrap leftover clay, including color-mixed clay, in a damp paper towel and keep in an airtight container or plastic bag, or wrap tightly in plastic wrap.

BASIC TECHNIQUES

Large balls: Roll the amount you will need on your work surface with the palm of your hand.

Ropes: Start with a ball and roll it back and forth with both hands to stretch it to the thickness you need.

Petals: Lightly roll a ball of clay in the palm of your hand, then press the ball with your thumb to the desired petal shape.

Flattening the clay: Use your roller to flatten the clay to the thickness you need, the same way you roll out dough.

"Ruffling" clay: Roll out the clay with one side thinner than the other. On the thinner side, use fingers to pull and then twist the clay.

Color mixing: To mix colors, pull and stretch the clay to get your colors mixed well. This is almost like stretching taffy.

BASIC LEAF

1 Using the base of your palm, roll a 1-inch diameter ball of green clay into a 1-inch teardrop.

2 Press teardrop onto textured side of leaf mold, pointing tip of leaf upward.

3 Spread clay to desired size and shape.

4 Detach beginning at wide end; grooves will be impressed onto clay.

5 Slightly twist and bend sides to give desired shape and form.

STEM

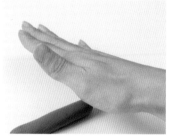   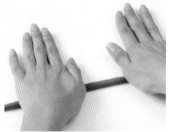

1 Roll 2-inch diameter ball of green clay into a 6-inch long rope.

2 Press #18-gauge wire into middle of rope.

3 Pinch top of clay around wire.

4 Starting from middle of wire, gently press and roll out clay, moving your hands out from middle to stretch clay. Continue rolling until wire is completely covered.

ATTACHING STEM TO FLOWER

1 Cut about 1 inch of clay off one end of wire. Stem should be completely dried.

2 Add glue to exposed wire and insert into dry flower.

3 Add a little clay to area where flower meets stem to finish.

COLOR MIXING

The Color Chart shows basic colors and proportions to use to achieve various colors for your projects. When making new colors, estimate the amount you'll need and then add colors in very small amounts as you knead the clay to get the exact shade you want.

For pastels, mix just a tiny pinch of colored clay into white clay.

PRIMARY

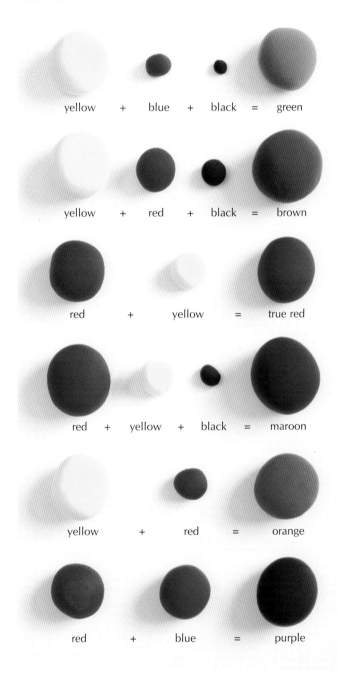

yellow   +   blue   +   black   =   green

yellow   +   red   +   black   =   brown

red   +   yellow   =   true red

red   +   yellow   +   black   =   maroon

yellow   +   red   =   orange

red   +   blue   =   purple

PASTELS

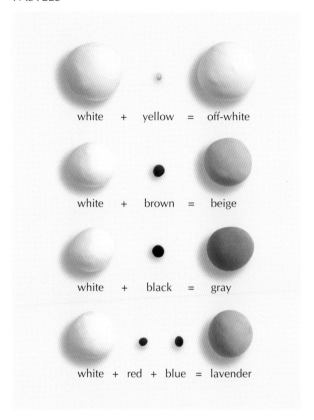

white + yellow = off-white

white + brown = beige

white + black = gray

white + red + blue = lavender

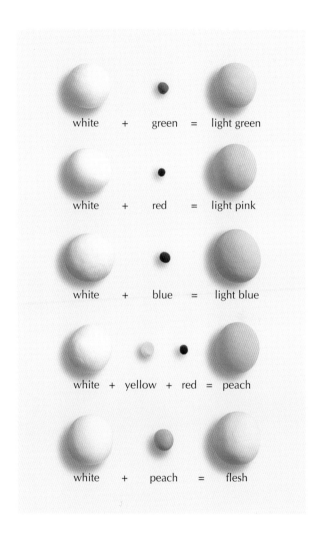

white + green = light green

white + red = light pink

white + blue = light blue

white + yellow + red = peach

white + peach = flesh

ROSEBUD—PETALS

1 Make seven 1-inch diameter balls.

2 Press each ball with your thumb to form petal shape.

3 Roll one petal from the edge to create the center of the bud.

4 Wrap second petal once around center of bud, keeping height of petals even.

5 Wrap third petal around second, overlapping it by about half. Slightly flare both edges of third petal, then pinch petals together at base.

6 Repeat step 5 with remaining petals, attaching all at base. Remove any excess clay remaining at base.

CALYX

1 Roll green clay into five ¹/₂-inch diameter balls.

2 Use rounded base of your palm to roll each ball into a 1¹/₄-inch teardrop.

3 Attach calyx leaves so they surround rosebud, with tips at same height as petal tops.

OPEN ROSE

1 Make fifteen petals as described in steps 1 and 2 for rosebud.

2 Roll one petal from the edge to form the center of the rose. Attach the second petal, keeping height of the two petals even, then pinch together at base. Slightly flare both edges of second petal.

3 Attach remaining petals one at a time the same way, overlapping each at halfway point of previous petal. Flare last petal completely so entire petal curves out.

TOOLS &
SPECIAL MATERIALS

Deco Detail Stick
Paintbrush
Acrylic Paint

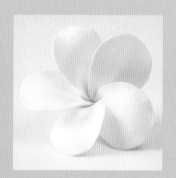

PLUMERIA

1 Roll white clay into five 1-inch diameter balls.

2 Use rounded base of your thumb to roll balls into a 1³/₄-inch thin teardrops.

3 Use your palm to slightly flatten petals.

4 Place flattened teardrop on your index finger, small end facing down. Hold thinner part of petal, press wider part with round Deco detail stick. With pressure mainly on upper portion of petal, roll stick back and forth to spread out petal. Repeat with remaining petals.

Pressed side of petal is the inside surface.

5 Fan petals, overlapping each about two-thirds over previous petal.

6 Twist petals together at base by turning left side of fan inward, then gently open petals.

7 Turn base of flower with your left hand and pull on petal edges to create an outward curve on each petal.

8 Tear away any excess clay at base. Let dry completely before painting.

9 To paint, wet brush, mix acrylic paint, then pick up some color and add to center of flower. Dry brush with paper towel. Then, starting from center of flower, use brush to bring paint out to middle of petal.

Daffodil

TOOLS & SPECIAL MATERIALS
Deco Detail Stick
Toothpick

DAFFODIL

TRUMPET

1 Mix yellow and white clay with a tiny bit of red to form 1-inch ball.

2 Use rounded base of your thumb to roll ball into 1¼-inch teardrop.

3 Place a tiny bit of flattened off-white clay on the larger side of teardrop.

4 Insert angled end of Deco detail stick about half-way into larger end of teardrop. With index finger as a base, use detail stick to roll out clay to form trumpet opening.

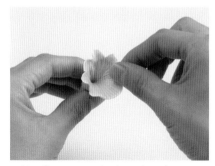

5 Use fingers to twist the edge of trumpet. Set aside.

PETALS

1 Roll off-white clay into six 1-inch diameter balls.

2 Use rounded base of your thumb to roll balls into 1¼-inch teardrops, then use fingers to sharpen larger ends into tips.

3 Flatten teardrops with fingertips to form petals. Thin edges with round Deco detail stick.

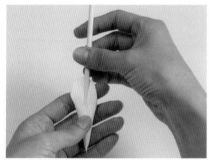

4 Use angled end of Deco detail stick to create texture on petal tops.

5 Fan petals, overlapping each about two-thirds over previous petal.

6 Twist petals together at base by turning left side of fan inward, then gently open petals.

7 Make an opening with angled end of Deco detail stick and insert trumpet in middle of petals. Use angled end of detail stick to help attach trumpet to petals.

STAMEN

1 Mix a little orange clay and make five tiny threads. Place threads together and use toothpick to insert into trumpet middle.

Gerbera Daisy

TOOLS & SPECIAL MATERIALS

Plastic Texture Brush
Scissors
Deco Detail Stick

CENTER

1 Roll light green clay into 1³/₄-inch diameter ball.

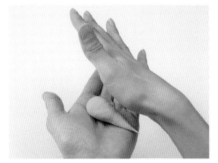

2 Use rounded base of your thumb to roll ball into 1¹/₂-inch teardrop.

3 Use plastic texture brush to add texture to top of teardrop. Set aside.

STAMEN

1 Mix a green slightly darker than the center and form into 1³/₄-inch diameter ball. Roll ball into 3-inch rope, then flatten one end.

2 Mix tiny bit of off-white and roll into a long, skinny rope. Place next to the flattened end of green rope, then press together.

3 Starting at one end of rope, make cut halfway into clay. Continue making cuts as close as possible until you reach the end.

PETALS

4 Wrap stamen around center, squeezing slightly and placing one-third of the stamen higher than the center. Continue to wrap around the center 2-3 times.

1 Make twenty-five balls, any color, about 1/2-inch diameter.

2 Use rounded base of your thumb to roll balls into 2-inch teardrops.

3 Flatten teardrops with angled-end Deco detail stick, then roll out to form petals, leaving the bottom half thicker than the top half.

4 Attach each petal around center of daisy, keeping tops of petals about 1-inch above center. If desired, add another layer of petals.

Lilac

TOOLS & SPECIAL MATERIALS

Scissors
Toothpick
#30-Gauge Wire
Floral Tape

LILAC

BUD

1 Make ¼-inch ball; roll into teardrop.

2 Cut larger end of teardrop in half, then cut each side in half again.

3 Close up to create bud.

OPEN FLOWER

1 Follow steps 1 and 2 above. Use your index finger as a base and roll toothpick to open each petal.

2 Before flowers dry, attach 3-inch length of #30-gauge wire with glue.

3 When dried, wrap wire with floral tape.

4 Tape flowers together to create a bunch.

Hibiscus

TOOLS & SPECIAL MATERIALS

Leaf Mold
Deco Detail Stick
#18-Gauge Wire
Scissors
Pliers

HIBISCUS

PETALS

1 Roll clay into five 1¼-inch diameter balls; form into 2¼-inch teardrops.

2 Place teardrop on leaf mold, narrow point of drop toward bottom of mold. Press clay onto mold, keeping center raised while flattening outer edges. Peel petal off mold.

3 Use fingertips to thin outer edge, then twist outer edge to create a frilled effect.

4 Fan petals, overlapping each about two-thirds over previous petal.

5 Twist petals together at base by turning left side of fan inward.

STAMEN

6 Make hole in center of flower with angled end of Deco detail stick. Shape petals, bending them outward so center of flower is raised above outer edge. Cut away excess clay at bottom of flower. Set aside.

1 Cover a 2-inch piece of #18-gauge wire with clay. Use same method for flower stems.

2 Form tiny piece of clay into small teardrop to make tip. Attach tip to end of stamen.

3 Cut tip with scissors at an angle from bottom to top to form little buds. Let dry.

4 Use pliers to curve upper part of finished stamen ¾ inches from top, then insert stamen into center of flower with glue.

Peony

PEONY

1 Using one color of clay, roll ten balls to slightly less than 1-inch diameter and ten balls to slightly larger than 1-inch diameter. Form balls into 2¹/₂-inch teardrops.

2 Place large end of teardrop in your palm, then press and spread top of clay to form petal.

3 Pinch and thin outer edge of petal, then slightly twist edge to create a frilled effect.

4 With petal in cup of your hand, press middle with finger to curve petal inward.

5 Fan five small petals, cup face up, overlapping each about two-thirds over previous petal.

6 Twist petals together at base by turning left side of fan inward, with last petal overlapping first.

7 Add remaining five small petals, inserting about half in front the last one.

8 Attach a large petal, keeping it at same height as the bud. Continue to attach remaining large petals the same way, overlapping each at the halfway point of previous petal.

Orchid

TOOLS & SPECIAL MATERIALS

Deco Detail Stick
Leaf Mold

ORCHID

PETALS

1 Make five 1-inch diameter balls; form into 2-inch teardrops. With index finger, roll end of teardrop in palm of hand, then lengthen and sharpen larger end.

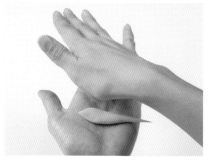

2 Press teardrop in palm of hand to flatten a little.

3 Flatten teardrops with fingertips to form petals.

4 Using index finger as a base, gently press and spread petal using round Deco detail stick. Repeat with the remaining petals.

LIP

1 Make one 1-inch ball in different color than petals and form into teardrop slightly over 1½-inch. Place on leaf mold with narrow end of teardrop down. Press and spread clay with fingers.

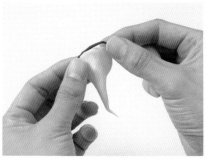

2 Add a different color to tip and place them back on the mold and press to join.

3 Peel petal off mold. Pinch and flatten outer edge, then slightly twist edge to create a frilled effect.

4 Place lip in cup of your hand and press center with your index finger to curve it inward.

5 Make small teardrop with darker-colored clay.

ASSEMBLY

6 Place in center to form stamen.

1 On either side of lip, attach two petals so they do not overlap.

2 Attach remaining three petals between the two petals and the lip, then evenly spread out petals.

Stephanotis

TOOLS & SPECIAL MATERIALS

Scissors
Deco Detail Stick
Toothpick

1 Make 1-inch diameter ball; form into 2¼-inch teardrop.

2 Use scissors to cut larger end of teardrop slightly off center about ¾-inch deep. Cut smaller piece in half and larger piece into three parts.

3 With index finger as base, gently roll out each section with toothpick to form petals.

4 Use round Deco detail stick to enlarge opening in center of flower.

5 Use angled Deco detail stick to add texture to flower.

6 Pinch off any excess clay at base of flower.

Pakalana

TOOLS & SPECIAL MATERIALS

Scissors
Toothpick
Deco Detail Stick

1   Make green ball slightly smaller than
    ¹/₂-inch diameter; form into ³/₄-inch
    teardrop.

2   Make yellow-green ¹/₁₆-inch diameter
    ball; flatten and place on larger end of
    teardrop. Gently press together.

3   Use scissors to cut larger end of
    teardrop slightly off center about
    ¹/₄-inch deep. Cut smaller piece in
    half and larger piece into three parts.

4   Use toothpick to gently roll out each
    section to form petals.

5   Insert round end of Deco detail stick in
    middle of flower to open.

6   Roll angled end of Deco detail stick on
    each petal.

Calla Lily

TOOLS & SPECIAL MATERIALS

Scissors
#18-Gauge Wire
Plastic Texture Brush
Roller
Cutter
Deco Detail Stick

CALLA LILY

STEM/STAMEN

1 Cut off 2 inches of clay from a stem that is dry.

2 Mix yellow clay for stamen and make a small rope. Insert uncovered wire into stamen.

3 Use plastic texture brush to add texture to stamen. Set aside to dry.

FLOWER

1 Use white clay to make 2-inch diameter ball and form into a teardrop shape.

2 With long roller, roll clay flat about 1/8-inch thick.

3 Use cutter to cut out teardrop shape.

4 Flatten petal edge by rolling round Deco detail stick on edge only.

5 Wrap petal around stem where stamen meets stem.

6 Wrap left side first then right, overlapping left.

7 Open petal sides then remove any excess clay and smooth bottom of petal.

Poinsettia

TOOLS &
SPECIAL MATERIALS

Artifical Stamen (gold ball)
Floral Tape
Leaf Mold

1 Bind three to five gold balls with floral tape. (Already attached to wire, available at craft stores.)

2 Mix red, yellow, and white clay to make a true red. Use a small piece of red clay to create a rope; wrap around ball cluster.

3 Use remaining red clay to make three 1/2-inch diameter balls, three 3/4-inch diameter balls, and five balls a little less than 1-inch diameter. Form balls into teardrops.

4 Press teardrops onto textured side of leaf mold, tip pointing up.

5 Add three small leaves around gold balls, slightly higher than ball.

6 Add three medium leaves in between smaller ones, slightly higher than them.

7 Add five large leaves around medium ones, slightly higher than them.

Long Stem Rose

TOOLS & SPECIAL MATERIALS

#24-Gauge Wire
Scissors
Floral Tape
Ribbon
Glue

LONG STEM ROSE

1 Make roses and stems and let dry completely.

2 Make 3 leaves and attach 3-inch piece of #24-gauge wire. Add glue to one end of wire and push one-third of way into middle of leaf.

3 Pull extra clay about 1 inch down and around stem. Let dry.

4 Cut about 1 inch of clay from stem to expose wire and add glue.

5 Insert exposed wire into rose.

6 When dry, wrap stem with floral tape starting at base of rose and moving down stem.

7 Wrap two leaves together with floral tape. Cover other leaf the same way.

8 Place leaves on stem and wrap together with floral tape.

9 Tie three to five roses together with ribbon.

Valentine's Day

Valentine Gift Box

TOOLS & SPECIAL MATERIALS

#20-Gauge Wire
Floral Tape
Water Glue
Ribbon

VALENTINE GIFT BOX

PREPARATION

Make one large peony, one medium peony, and five roses. Decorate box with ribbon.

HEARTS

1 Mix white and red clay to make different shades of pinks. Make two 1-inch diameter balls, form into 6-inch teardrops, then shape each into one side of heart.

2 Repeat step 1 to make the other side of the heart. Use water glue to attach the sides together.

3 After clay dries, glue 3-inch #20-gauge wire to bottom of heart and wrap with floral tape. Repeat steps 1-3 to make hearts in different sizes. Paint decorative elements on hearts, if desired.

BOX COVER

1 Mix green clay and attach to box using glue. Spread clay edges and press down. This will be a base for attaching your flowers.

2 Glue flowers to base, starting with largest flowers (peony). Add your flowers to the base using glue. Place your roses between the peonies. Attach wires to rose bottoms for added height, if necessary.

3 Make single or double loop with ribbon. Attach bottom of ribbon to 2-inch #20-gauge wire with floral tape. Attach two to three 7- to 8-inch strips of ribbon to wire in the same way.

4 Arrange hearts and ribbons in between the flowers.

Decorated
Egg

TOOLS & SPECIAL MATERIALS

Roller
Styrofoam Egg
Plastic Texture Brush
Water Glue
#20-Gauge Wire
Ribbon

DECORATED EGG

EGG

1 Roll out clay to 1/8-inch thickness.

2 Cover Styrofoam egg with clay.

3 Use plastic texture brush to add texture to entire egg.

FLOWERS

1 Make five 1/4-inch diameter balls. Shape balls into 1-inch teardrops and flatten with fingers, making petals uniformly thin.

2 Place petals on egg to make flower.

3 Use plastic texture brush to add texture. (If clay begins to dry, use water-based glue to help it adhere to egg.) Place flattened pinhead-size yellow ball on middle of flower and add texture. Add more flowers of desired color and shape.

4 Make 1-inch clay rope, attach to egg, press down, and add texture. (Attach longer ropes the same way.)

5 When completely dry, attach a small piece of #20-gauge wire to the ribbon and attach bow to top of egg.

Easter

Basket with Flowers

TOOLS & SPECIAL MATERIALS

#18-Gauge Wire
Roller
Small Texture Brush
Cutter
Styrofoam
Paper Towel
Scissors
Glue

BASKET WITH FLOWERS

PREPARATION

Make flowers, let dry, then attach 3-inch piece of #18-gauge wire to each.

HANDLE

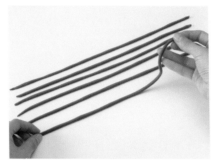

1 Mix brown clay to use for basket and handle. Make six thin 7-inch clay ropes.

2 Place three ropes next to each other, then two on top of them, then last one on top in a pyramid.

3 Place palms on ends. Twist clay, moving one hand forward and the other back, two or three times to make rope tight.

4 Pinch ends so ropes stay together. Shape handle and set aside to dry.

BASKET

1 Make two clay sheets using roller; flatten to $1/4$-inch thickness. Use small texture brush to add "weave" marks, starting from top and moving from one end to other.

2 Cut off excess clay to make 7-by-3-inch sheets.

3 Cut 4-by-2-inch rectangle from 1-inch thick Styrofoam. Place one sheet of flattened clay on each side of Styrofoam, tucking clay under to cover bottom.

4 Pinch seams to join clay together. Place paper towel inside to add support and body.

5 Make rope 16-inches long, 3/4-inch diameter. Attach around top of basket.

6 Use scissors to make rope lines and add texture to rope.

7 Attach handle with glue to basket. Add support under top of handle and let dry overnight.

FILLING BASKET

1 When basket is dry, add green clay to cover Styrofoam. Glue flowers inside. Add any desired decorative items.

TOOLS &
SPECIAL MATERIALS

Deco Detail Stick
Glue
Toothpicks
Scissors

CHICK AND BUNNY

CHICK

1 Make light yellow clay about 2¹/₂-inches in diameter; set aside 1¹/₄-inch ball for head and wings.

2 Body: Use light yellow clay to make a short, fat cone; pinch and pull pointed end to make tail; flatten top and bottom a little.

3 Head: Make ³/₄-inch ball and attach to top of body. Smooth joint between head and body with Deco detail stick and water glue.

4 Wings: Make two ¹/₂-inch balls with reserved clay; form into teardrops; flatten slightly and glue to body.

5 Add yellow and red to remaining clay to make a light orange color for beak, legs and feet. Beak: Make two tiny teardrops, flatten a little and add to head. Make two small brown balls and place on either side of beak for eyes.

6 Feet: Make 3 small ropes and place them together.

7 Legs: Cut 2 toothpicks into 1¹/₂-inch lengths and cover with light orange clay. Press toothpicks into feet and let dry; insert legs with feet into bottom of body with glue.

BUNNY

1 Mix light brown clay about 2¹/₂-inches in diameter. Body: Use 1-inch of ball and form into long cone. Trim bottom at an angle.

2 Legs: Make two balls a little over ¹/₂-inch; form into teardrops; bend smaller ends to form feet.

3 Glue legs to body.

4 Arms: Make two ¹/₂-inch balls; form into teardrops; pinch smaller ends to form hands, bend in middle for elbows; glue to body.

5 Head: Make fat cone shape with 1-inch ball of clay; pull clay on smaller side to form nose. Push toothpick about halfway into body, put head on toothpick.

6 Ears: Make two balls a little larger than ¹/₂-inch and form into teardrops; flatten teardrops and glue to top of head.

7 Add some pink to the inside of the ears. Use a toothpick to add "stitches" on edge.

8 Nose: Make one tiny ball of brown clay; glue to face. Eyes: Make little dimples with Deco detail stick.

9 Add tiny bit of clay for eyes.

10 Finish with ribbon: Flatten clay and cut small strips; attach around neck; make two small loops for bow and attach to ribbon.

Lei

TOOLS & SPECIAL MATERIALS

Scissors
String
Lei Needle

LEI

1 Make thirty-five plumeria. Let dry completely. Leave $3/4$ to 1-inch clay at flower bottoms; cut off excess.

2 Cut 50-inch piece of string. String flowers with lei needle.

3 When lei is desired length, tie ends together.

Graduation

Haku Lei

TOOLS & SPECIAL MATERIALS

Raffia
Greenery
Floral Tape
#30-Gauge Wire
Glue

HAKU LEI

PREPARATION

Make fifty to sixty rosebuds, twenty stephanotis, twenty pakalana, twenty pakalana bud clusters, and twelve lilac clusters (in threes). Amount of flowers may vary according to the size and fullness desired. Gather various sprigs of leaves and ferns for additional decorations in lei. Attach 3-inch #30-gauge wire with glue to flowers and items. Wrap with floral tape.

1   Cut three strands of raffia about 1 foot longer than desired length of lei and braid together.

2   Tie another strand of raffia to beginning of braided strand, about 1 to 2 inches from top (leaving enough room to tie ends together). This strand will be used to secure the flowers and leaves to the haku. Place flowers and green sprigs onto braided strand and wrap raffia strand around items securely to braid.

3   Add fern greenery to back of lei, in alternating angles.

4   Repeat steps 2 and 3 till you reach desired length. Keep at least 2 inches of the braided raffia free at the bottom to tie together with the beginning.

5   Tie raffia strand into a knot onto the braid at the end of the lei.

Wedding
Hand-Tied
Bouquet

TOOLS &
SPECIAL MATERIALS

Floral Tape
#24-Gauge Wire
Artificial Leaves
Ribbon
Pin

BASKET WITH FLOWERS

PREPARATION

Make flowers, let dry, then attach 3-inch piece of #18-gauge wire to each.

HANDLE

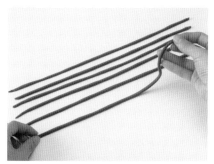

1 Mix brown clay to use for basket and handle. Make six thin 7-inch clay ropes.

2 Place three ropes next to each other, then two on top of them, then last one on top in a pyramid.

3 Place palms on ends. Twist clay, moving one hand forward and the other back, two or three times to make rope tight.

4 Pinch ends so ropes stay together. Shape handle and set aside to dry.

BASKET

1 Make two clay sheets using roller; flatten to 1/4-inch thickness. Use small texture brush to add "weave" marks, starting from top and moving from one end to other.

2 Cut off excess clay to make 7-by-3-inch sheets.

3 Cut 4-by-2-inch rectangle from 1-inch thick Styrofoam. Place one sheet of flattened clay on each side of Styrofoam, tucking clay under to cover bottom.

4 Pinch seams to join clay together. Place paper towel inside to add support and body.

5 Make rope 16-inches long, 3/4-inch diameter. Attach around top of basket.

6 Use scissors to make rope lines and add texture to rope.

7 Attach handle with glue to basket. Add support under top of handle and let dry overnight.

FILLING BASKET

1 When basket is dry, add green clay to cover Styrofoam. Glue flowers inside. Add any desired decorative items.

HAND-TIED BOUQUET

1 Make desired flowers with stems and let dry. Place three main flowers together and wrap with floral tape.

2 Keep adding flowers in between at same height until reaching outer edge, then place additional flowers a little lower to create oval shape. Wrap bunch together with floral tape.

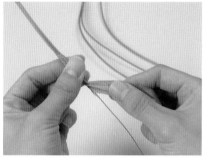

3 Wrap floral tape around 3-inch #24-gauge wire for leaves.

4 Add artificial leaves to bouquet and wrap stems together once more with floral tape.

5 Tie with ribbon and pin to finish.

Shadow Box with Dress

TOOLS & SPECIAL MATERIALS

Roller
Texture Brush
Deco Detail Stick
Scissors
Styrofoam
Glue

SHADOW BOX WITH DRESS

PREPARATION

Dress size below fits
8-by-10-inch shadow box.
If desired, cover back of
frame with material.

LACE FOR DRESS

1 Make two clay ropes each
12-by-³/₄-inch wide. Flatten
with roller to ¹/₁₆-inch thick.

2 Use angled Deco detail stick to
create detail; press stick down
and push clay to side, then
push bottom of clay up
to create scalloped edge. As
shown in picture 3 of dress
section.

3 Pull bottom of scalloped part to
make clay thinner.

4 Gather top part of lace.

5 Place clay down and press
down from middle to top.

6 Cut off excess clay at top.
Set aside.

DRESS

1 Roll ³/₄ package of white clay
to ¹/₈-inch thickness, then cut
rectangle about 5-by-10 inches.
Roll clay again until it is ¹/₁₆-
inch thick.

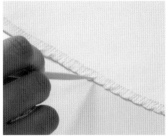

2 Press texture brush on one side to create ruffled bottom. Use angled Deco detail stick to push bottom of dress up to create a scalloped edge.

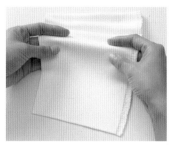

3 Place dress on lap and use fingers to pull and gather clay.

4 Make small gathers at top of dress and pinch together.

5 Cut Styrofoam piece to shape of dress, place under dress to help keep shape.

BODY

6 Use glue or water glue to attach lace under bottom of dress.

1 Add clay under top of dress to create body.

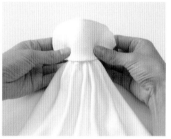

2 Make clay log and flatten with roller to 3-inch width. Cut off bottom and sides to fit around body.

3 Cover body with clay and cut excess off back.

4 Cut off excess clay at top then smooth and create bustline.

5 Make a little hole in top of body.

6 Make two skinny 3/4-inch long ropes for dress straps. Glue on. Add other accessories, such as flowers, gloves, veil, etc.

TOOLS & SPECIAL MATERIALS

Styrofoam Ball
Cutter
Deco Detail Stick
Acrylic Paint
Paintbrush

PUMPKIN

BODY

1 Mix orange clay and make eight to nine 1½-inch diameter balls. Use palms to make large teardrops, with middle fairly large and ends skinnier.

2 Cut small slice off top and bottom of 3-inch diameter Styrofoam ball.

3 Place teardrops next to each other on ball; press clay at top and bottom to join ends together.

4 Use round Deco detail stick to join segments of clay.

STEM

1 Mix brown clay, form into ¾-inch diameter ball. Roll one end between fingers to pull clay. Flatten other end.

2 Attach to top of pumpkin.

FACE

1 When dry, draw pumpkin face with acrylic paint.

Trick-or-Treat Bag

TOOLS & SPECIAL MATERIALS

Cutter
Pliers
#18- & #24-Gauge Wire
Scissors
Deco Detail Stick
Toothpick
Ribbon
Wire Rope

TRICK-OR-TREAT BAG

BAG

SPIDER

1 Make pumpkin; let dry. Cut out about 3/4-inch of inside of pumpkin.

1 Legs: Cut eight 3-inch #24-gauge wire pieces. Cover with black clay using same method for making flower stems.

2 With scissors, make angled cuts in clay to create "hairy" effect. Let dry, then bend to spider leg shape.

3 Body/head: Make 1½-inch diameter black ball for body and flatten a little; make 3/4-inch diameter ball for head.

4 Use Deco detail stick and water-based glue to smooth joint between head and body. Set aside.

5 Glue legs to body.

6 Add tiny balls for eyes and nose. Make mouth with skinny rope.

GHOST

1 Make 1½-inch ball; form into teardrop shape.

2 Flatten and pull out each side to make hands.

3 Add a little piece of black clay for eyes and mouth.

JACK-O-LANTERN

1 Make 1½-inch diameter orange ball. Flatten a little and pull clay at top to make stem.

2 Press Deco detail stick into clay to create pumpkin's ridges.

3 Roll piece of clay, fairly thick. Cut out eyes, nose, and mouth.

4 Attach to jack-o-lantern.

ASSEMBLY

1 Mix orange clay and cover Styrofoam.

2 Insert 2-inch #18 gauge wire in bottom of dried items. Arrange items in pumpkin and attach with glue.

3 If desired, attach wire rope for handle and decorate with ribbon.

Wreath

TOOLS & SPECIAL MATERIALS

Glue
Ribbon

WREATH

1 Make poinsettias: Three large (one white, two red), two small red and two small white. Make 3-inch diameter brown ball and roll out six different sizes of rope.

2 Place two ropes together, place hands on each end of rope and twist, moving one hand up and the other down.

3 Join ends together to form a circle. Add remaining ropes of clay to make vine thicker.

4 Cut bottom of poinsettias flat and glue to top of vines.

5 When dry, add decorative items, such as ribbon, twisted rope, etc.

Santa Ornament

TOOLS & SPECIAL MATERIALS

Styrofoam Cone
Box Cutter
Scissors
Deco Detail Stick
Toothpick
Needle
Water Glue
Texture Brush, Small
Cutter

SANTA ORNAMENT

BODY

1 Cut about 1 inch off top of 6-inch Styrofoam cone.

2 Mix together ¾ package red clay and ⅕ package yellow clay and same amount of yellow for white. (Not ⅕ package white but same amount of clay as yellow.) Make log and roll to ¼ -inch thickness with long roller. Cover Styrofoam with clay.

3 Cut off excess clay where ends meet and smooth out the seam.

4 Use fingers to stretch clay at base of Styrofoam to cover bottom. Remove any excess.

ARM/HANDS

1 Use some of remaining clay to make two balls a little larger than 1-inch diameter; form into teardrops and flatten a little.

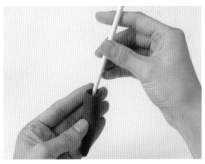

2 Use round Deco detail stick to create an opening on the larger side of the teardrop.

3 Use toothpick to make bend lines in middle of teardrop, then slightly bend teardrop to form arms.

4 Make two ¹/₂–inch diameter black balls; form into teardrops and flatten.

5 Use scissors to cut V shape in clay to form mitten.

FACE

6 Use fingers to make end of mittens skinnier; insert in arms.

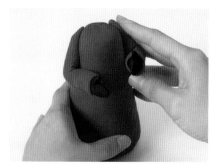

7 Glue arms to the top sides of cone.

1 Make 1¹/₂-inch ball of flesh tone clay; remove ¹/₂-inch ball and add a little more yellow and red for cheeks and nose. Put aside tiny bit of the flesh-tone clay for eyes, then roll remaining clay into a ball. Push toothpick halfway into top of the Styrofoam cone and place ball on toothpick.

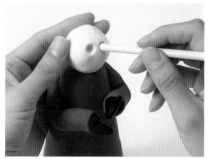

2 Use Deco detail stick to create dimples for eyes a little above halfway mark of ball.

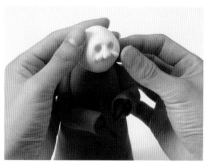

3 Use darker flesh tone clay to make a teardrop for nose. Place in-between eyes. Make two smaller flesh tone teardrops and place on sides of nose for cheeks.

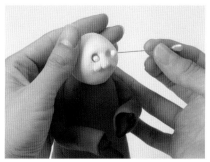

4 Use flesh-tone clay set aside in step 1 to make two balls; place in dimples for the eyes. Use needle to open them up.

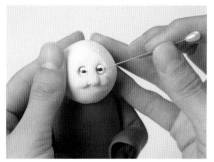

5 Make two tiny black balls and place in middle of eyes for iris, then four even smaller blue balls to go on both sides of the black.

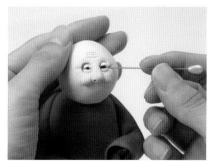

6 Using a needle add some frown lines to forehead. Add holes for nostrils.

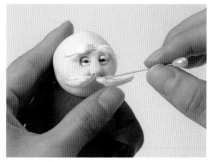

7 Make long, white teardrops to create eyebrows and mustache. Use water glue to attach to face.

8 Make different length white teardrops for beard and add to head. Texture brush can be used to create lines in beard.

9 Continue adding different lengths of white to his beard. Now add a hole for mouth using the needle.

HAT

1 Roll leftover red clay into a little less than 1/4-inch thickness, cut bottom into a curved shape.

2 Cover top of head with red clay and cut off excess. Bend top of hat slightly.

ROBE TRIM

1 Make white rope and flatten a little. Use water glue to attach rope pieces around bottom of cone, down middle of robe, around sleeves, and around rim of hat.

BOOTS

2 Make small white ball and attach to tip of hat. Use texture brush to make ropes look "fluffy."

1 Make two black 1-inch diameter balls and form into teardrops. With teardrops on flat surface, press the middle with fingers, pushing smaller end of teardrop up.

2 Push toothpick into top of boot and let dry.

3 Glue to bottom of cone.

CHRISTMAS TREE

1 Mix dark green clay and form into cone shape. Pull clay down and out with small texture brush, beginning at bottom and going completely around cone.

2 At about ¼-inch from top of tree, pull clay up instead of down.

3 Glue tree in Santa's hands.

Using the technique for Santa's face and Christmas tree, you can also make pins, ornaments, etc.